The Farmyard
in Patchwork and Appliqué

Hélène Martin

For my friend Martine Chan, who was the inspiration behind this book and without whom none of this would have been possible.

To my family: my parents, my husband and my son, who have remained supportive and enthusiastic throughout.

First published in the UK in 2005 by
David & Charles
Brunel House Newton Abbot Devon
www.davidandcharles.co.uk
David & Charles is a subsidiary of F+W (UK) Ltd.,
an F+W Publications Inc. company

A catalogue record for this book is available from the British Library.

ISBN 0 7153 2139 0

Paperback edition published in North America in 2005 by
KP Books, an F+W Publications Inc. company
700 East State Street, Iola, WI 54990
715-445-2214/888-457-2873
www.krause.com

A catalog record for this book is available from the Library of Congress: 2005922944

ISBN 0-89689-257-3

Copyright ©LTA – Meta-Editions, 2003
Originally published as *Appliqué & Patchwork, Bestiare de la Ferme* by LTA – Meta-Editions, 2003

Printed in Singapore by KHL Printing Co Pte Ltd

INTRODUCTION

The patchwork bedspread featured in this book takes the form of a delightful and elegant farmyard miscellany made using an assortment of printed fabrics in blues, browns and yellows. What a perfect opportunity to use up those odds and ends of fabric!

The book contains a comprehensive diagram of the quilt and its motifs, all of which are individually numbered, along with practical advice on materials and equipment, cutting, sewing and appliqué techniques.

There are also easy-to-follow step-by-step instructions on creating and assembling your quilt.

And if making a large quilt is too time-consuming a project for you to take on, why not use the motifs in this book to make cushions, a bedside rug or a dog blanket instead? The possibilities are endless!

CONTENTS

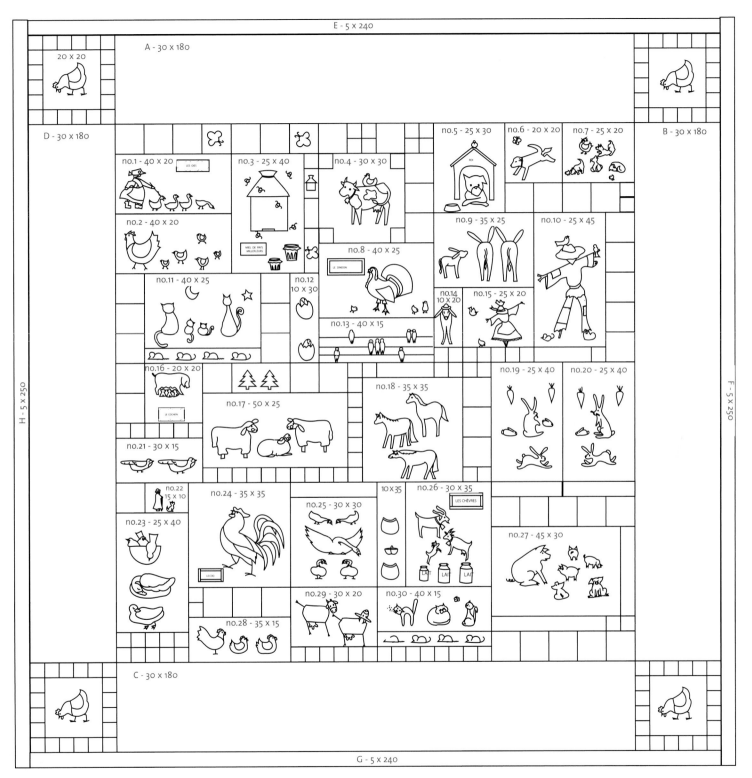

Note: All measurements given in centimetres. Refer to motif templates (pages 18–81) for Imperial measurements.

PRACTICAL HINTS AND TIPS

PRACTICAL HINTS AND TIPS

A ▪ Basic equipment

1 – WORKING WITH MOTIFS AND TEMPLATES

- **Graph paper** – the kind with 5mm (¼in) squares is ideal.
- **Ruler** marked in both centimetres and inches.
- **Plain paper** – large sheets for enlarging motifs to full size.
- **Tracing paper**.
- **Thin card** such as Bristol-board or sheets of acetate.
- **HB pencil** sharpened to a fine point to draw on paper.
- **Fabric markers** including a selection of dressmaker's pencils, air-erasable fabric markers and water-soluble fabric markers in various colours.
- **Scissors** to cut paper, card and acetate.

2 – CUTTING OUT YOUR FABRIC

- **Cutting mats** come in several sizes and are often marked with useful grids for cutting. If possible choose a large size, about 45 x 60cm (18 x 24in), and store flat.
- **Rotary cutter** is essential to cut straight lines with precision. The larger-diameter blades are for thick fabrics or several layers; the smaller are good for cutting round sharp curves. The blades can be sharpened or replaced.
- **Dressmaking shears** to cut out small pieces of appliqué fabric (never use them to cut out paper or card).
- **Quilter's rule** in thick clear acrylic, and marked with vertical and horizontal lines, for use with the rotary cutter and mat. The larger sizes also have diagonal lines.

3 – SEWING

- **Dressmaking shears**.
- **Very fine pins** (dressmaking or lace pins).
- **Sewing machine**.
- **Machine needles** of various sizes to match the fabrics.

To create the designs in this book, and the appliqué in particular, you need a sewing machine that can make a close, regular zigzag satin stitch. You will find it easier to work if you can regulate the pressure of the foot. If possible use an appliqué foot which is hinged and transparent and will accommodate a build-up of stitches underneath.

Note: A sewing machine will make your work a lot easier but it is not essential.

- **Sewing thread** in a range of colours. Use cotton with natural fabrics and synthetic threads with man-made fabrics.
- **Stranded embroidery silks** in a range of colours.
- **Hand-sewing needles** of various sizes for simple seams, embroidery and quilting.
- **Tissue paper** to place under the backing fabric when machining – you can buy a purpose-made material called Stitch and tear.
- **Fusible backing material** for stiffening fine fabrics such as Bondaweb.

B ▪ Patchwork tips

1 – PREPARING YOUR FABRIC

Fabrics should be washed and ironed before use. If the colours run in the wash, rinse the fabric through several times until the water runs clear.

Cotton is the easiest fabric to work with. The quilts shown in this book mainly use linen and cotton for the panel backgrounds and borders as well as for individual pieces. Synthetic materials and woollen fabrics have been used for some of the appliqué work to create special effects.

Wadding made from synthetic material will make the quilt easy to wash. Choose a thickness according to the effect you are trying to achieve. It is sometimes possible to reduce bulk by separating it into two sheets.

2 – CUTTING OUT YOUR FABRIC

Seam allowances will depend on the seam guide on your machine. The allowance is usually 1cm (½in). If you are given dimensions without a seam allowance, you should add 1cm (½in) all the way around the piece to be cut out. If you intend to make your patchwork by hand, you can reduce the seam allowance to 6mm (¼in).

Grain of the fabric is important. Always cut your squares and rectangles along the grain to prevent the fabric from pulling out of shape.

C ▪ Appliqué tips

1 – MACHINE APPLIQUE

- Enlarge the motif, if necessary, by hand or using a photocopier. Make two more photocopies for cutting out the templates.
- Select the fabrics for the background panel and motifs.
- Cut out the background panel to the required size, remembering to add seam allowances.
- Cut a piece of tissue paper (or Stitch and tear) to the same size as the background panel (optional).
- Using two of the photocopies, cut out card or acetate templates for all the pieces without seam allowances. You need two photocopies because some of the pieces overlap others (see sample motif page 14). Number the pieces on your reference photocopy and on your cut-out templates.
- Lay the templates out on the right side of the fabrics and draw around them using a fabric marker (see page 11).
- Cut the motifs out along the lines. Lay the fabric pieces out on the background panel, using the remaining drawing as a guide and overlapping as necessary. Pin them in place and tack.

Note: Avoid overhandling pieces with raw edges as they may fray.

- Select your thread colour, set your machine to satin zigzag stitch and place your needle as far as possible inside the piece to be appliquéd.

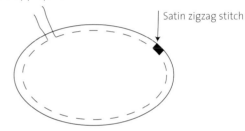

Satin zigzag stitch

- Adjust the pressure of the foot so that it is not as firm as for regular stitching. This will make it easier to guide your fabric and will prevent puckering.
- When you reach a corner keep the needle in the fabric, lift the foot and pivot the fabric around the needle. Make sure that you start your satin stitch from the correct side. For outside corners stop with the needle to the right, for inside corners stop with the needle to the left.
- To sew curved lines, gently turn your fabric as you sew. If the curve becomes more pronounced, lift the foot, turn the fabric slightly around the needle and then continue.

Sample motif

TURKEY FROM BORDER PANEL C

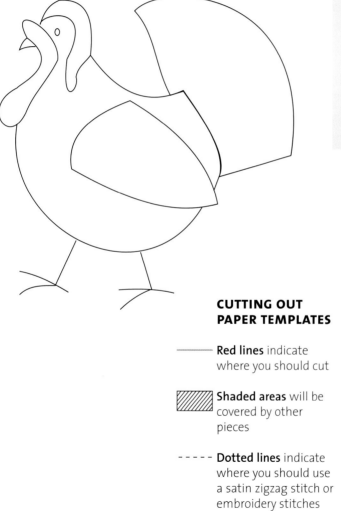

APPLIQUE KNOW-HOW

- Spray-starch and then steam-iron fabrics to add body before using them to make appliqué pieces.
- To add body to fine fabrics cut a piece of bonding fabric, such as Bondaweb, slightly larger than the motif and follow the manufacturer's instructions to fuse it to the fabric. Then cut out the motif.
- A sheet of tissue paper or Stitch and tear placed between the backing fabric and the bed of the machine prevents the fabric rucking up. Gently tear it away after stitching.

CUTTING OUT PAPER TEMPLATES

— **Red lines** indicate where you should cut

Shaded areas will be covered by other pieces

- - - - **Dotted lines** indicate where you should use a satin zigzag stitch or embroidery stitches

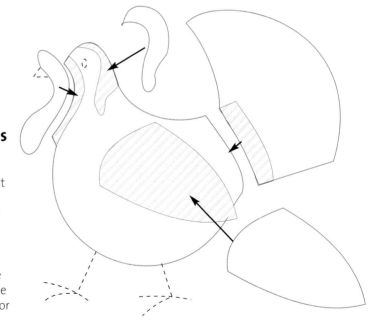

2 – HAND-SEWN APPLIQUE

Traditional method

- Enlarge the motif if necessary, make two photocopies and cut out the templates as for machine appliqué.
- Place the template on the right side of the fabric and draw round the edge. Mark a 6mm ($^1/_4$in) seam allowance round the motif and cut out just outside this line.
- Run a line of tiny stitches just outside the motif outline to prevent fraying and keep the piece in shape.
- Fold and finger-press the seam allowance to the wrong side along the drawn line, cutting notches where necessary in the curved edges.
- Place the pieces in position on the backing fabric and pin or tack in place.
- Choose a thread to match the fabric and slipstitch round the edge, inserting the needle just outside the fold and bringing it out just catching the edge of the piece. Continue all round the shape. Remove pins or tacking.

Note: If your motif is made up of several elements which overlap, like the turkey opposite, always position the lowest piece first.

Alternative method

- Work in the same way as for the traditional method but leave only a 3mm ($^1/_8$in) seam allowance when you cut out your fabric.
- Position the pieces and pin.
- Choose a thread colour to match your piece.
- Appliqué your piece using small slipstitches, pushing the 3mm ($^1/_8$in) seam allowance under as you sew using the point of your needle.

CHAPTER II
MOTIFS

GOOSE GIRL

Motif no.1

• Panel size:
40cm x 20cm
(16in x 8in)

• Enlarge diagram
by 200%

LES OIES

broderie
rouge
"les oies"

Fond bleu

Ecru

Taffias

Ecossais rouge

les oies

HEN AND CHICKS

Motif no.2

- Panel size:
  40cm x 20cm
  (16in x 8in)

- Enlarge diagram
  by 200%

BEEHIVE

Motif no.3

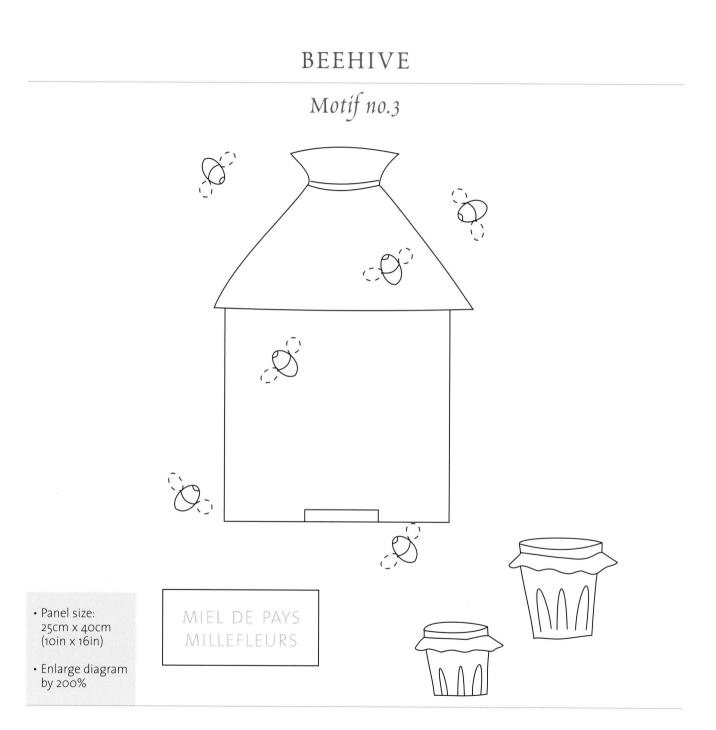

- Panel size:
  25cm x 40cm
  (10in x 16in)

- Enlarge diagram
  by 200%

MIEL DE PAYS
MILLEFLEURS

COW

Motif no.4

- Panel size: 30cm x 30cm (12in x 12in)
- Enlarge diagram by 200%

Poule perchée

Nakwenda

Rosalie

fond

REX THE DOG
Motif no.5

• Panel size:
25cm x 30cm
(10in x 12in)

• Shown actual
size

DOG

Motif no.6

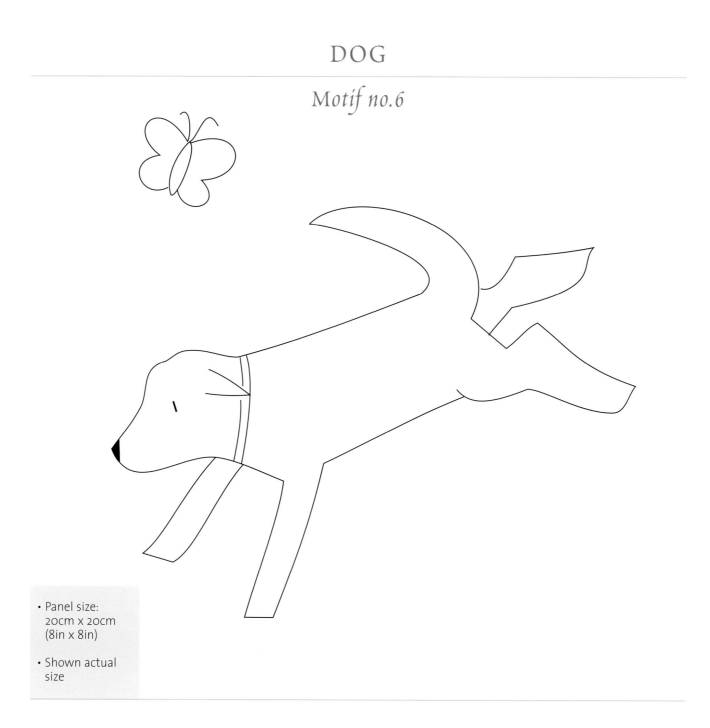

- Panel size:
  20cm x 20cm
  (8in x 8in)

- Shown actual
  size

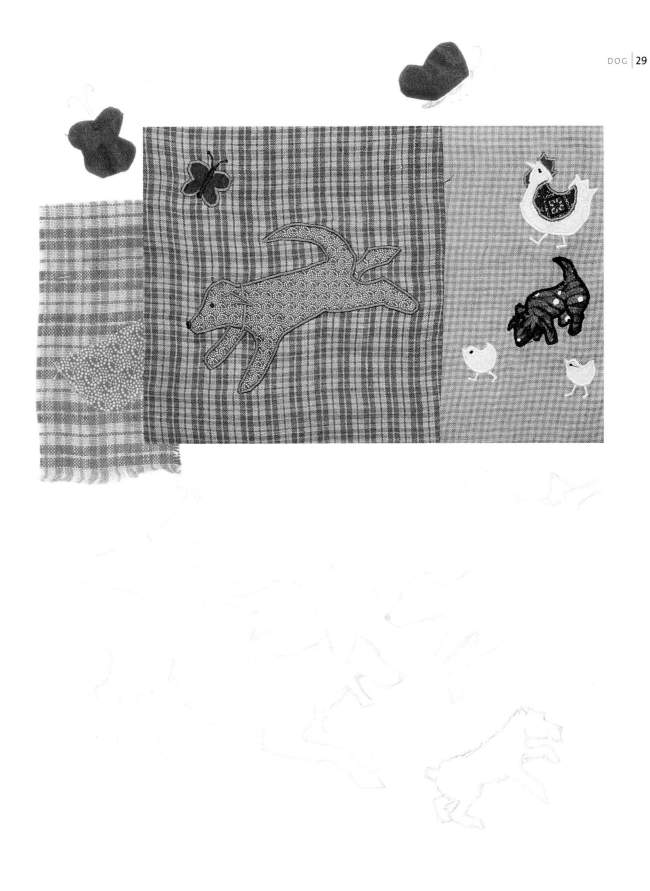

PUPPIES AND ROOSTER
Motif no.7

- Panel size:
  25cm x 20cm
  (10in x 8in)

- Shown actual
  size

TURKEY
Motif no.8

LE DINDON

- Panel size:
  40cm x 25cm
  (16in x 10in)

- Enlarge diagram
  by 200%

plumes
de l'aile
et de la
queue

plumes
du corps

LE DINDON

Etiquette imprimé
sur lin avec bordure
fleurie

Fond jaune safran

DONKEYS

Motif no.9

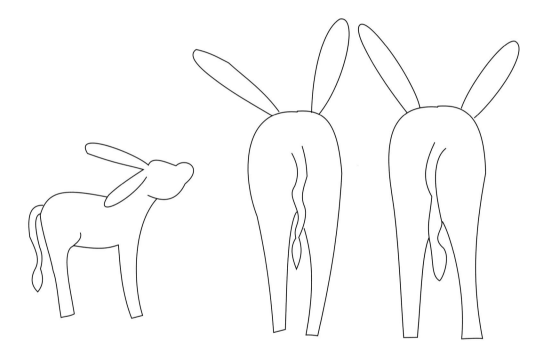

• Panel size:
  35cm x 25cm
  (14in x 10in)

• Enlarge diagram
  by 200%

LES ÂNES

gris de Provence

Fond

Père âne

Ânon

Maman âne

SCARECROW
Motif no.10

- Panel size:
  25cm x 45cm
  (10in x 18in)

- Enlarge diagram
  by 200%

CATS IN THE MOONLIGHT

Motif no.11

• Panel size:
40cm x 25cm
(16in x 10in)

• Enlarge diagram
by 200%

EGGS

Motif no.12

• Panel size:
  10cm x 30cm
  (4in x 12in)

• Shown actual
  size

jaune fleurs
pour l. tomussu
ot l'œuf

Fmd

SWALLOWS

Motif no.13

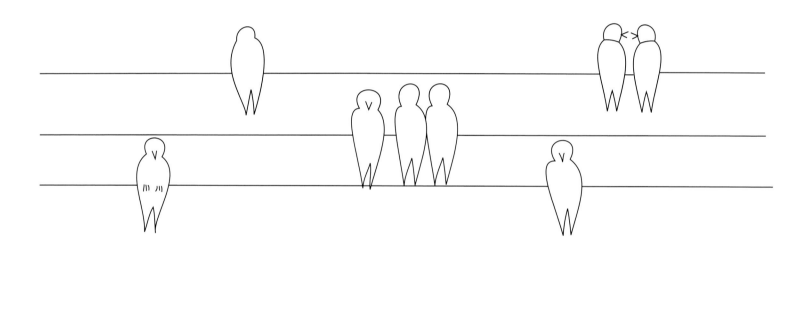

- Panel size:
  40cm x 15cm
  (16in x 6in)

- Enlarge diagram
  by 200%

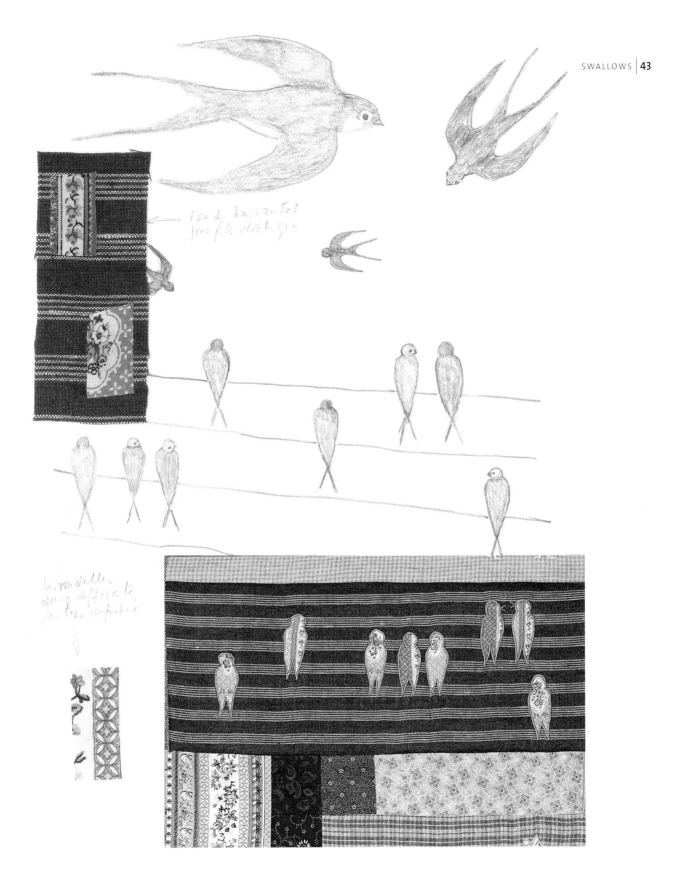

SAD DONKEY

Motif no.14

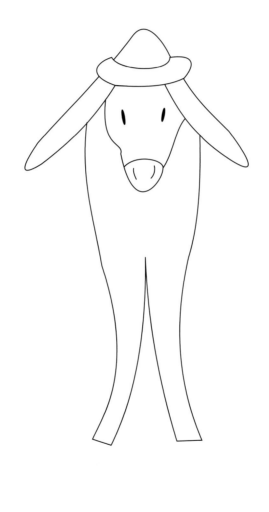

- Panel size:
  10cm x 20cm
  (4in x 8in)

- Shown actual
  size

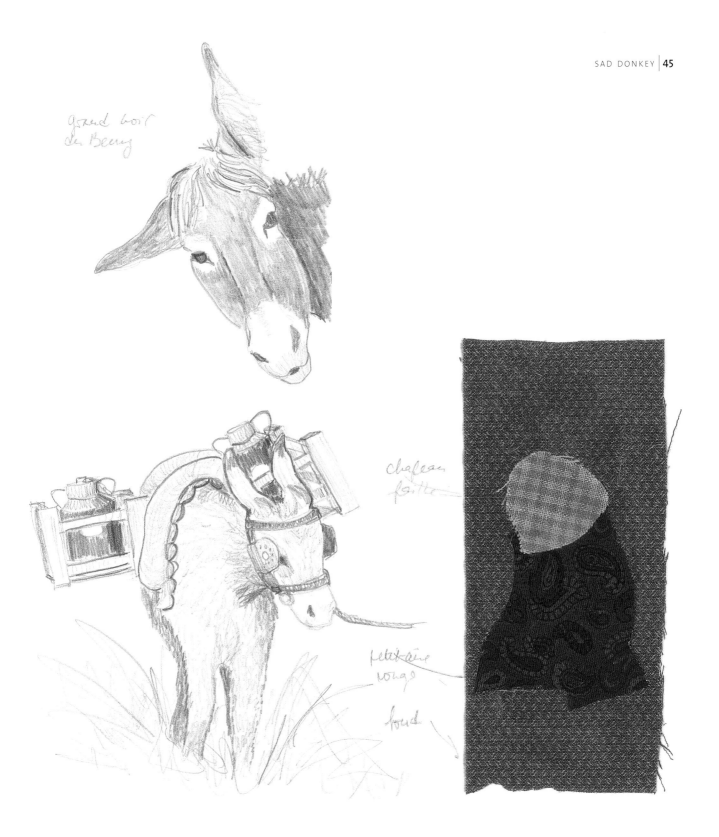

MRS SCARECROW

Motif no.15

- Panel size:
  25cm x 20cm
  (10in x 8in)

- Shown actual
  size

PIG WITH PIGLETS

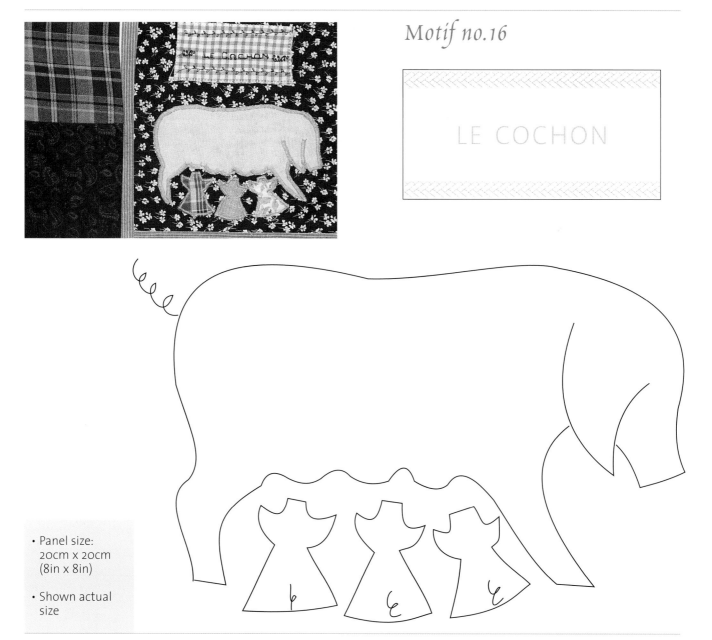

Motif no.16

LE COCHON

- Panel size:
  20cm x 20cm
  (8in x 8in)

- Shown actual
  size

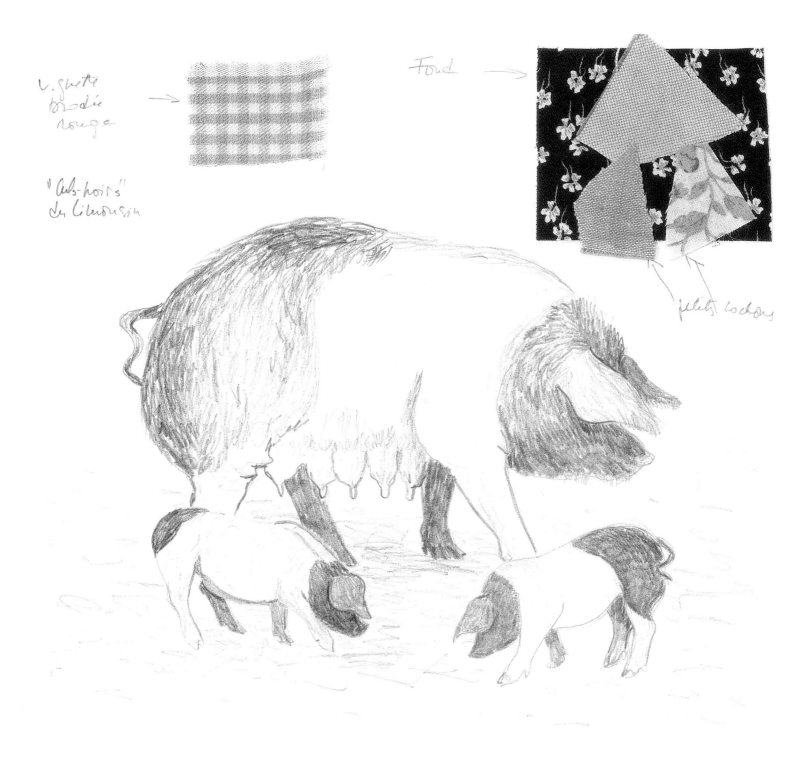

v. quote
brodée
rouge

" cul-noirs"
du Limousin

Fond →

petits cochons

SHEEP

Motif no.17

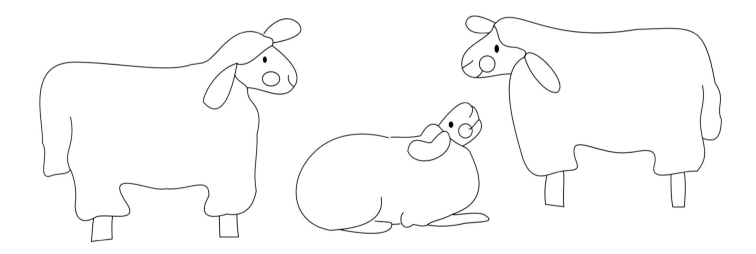

- Panel size:
  50cm x 25cm
  (20in x 10in)

- Enlarge diagram
  by 200%

HORSES

Motif no.18

• Panel size:
  35cm x 35cm
  (14in x 14in)

• Enlarge diagram
  by 200%

RABBITS FACE TO FACE

Motif no.19

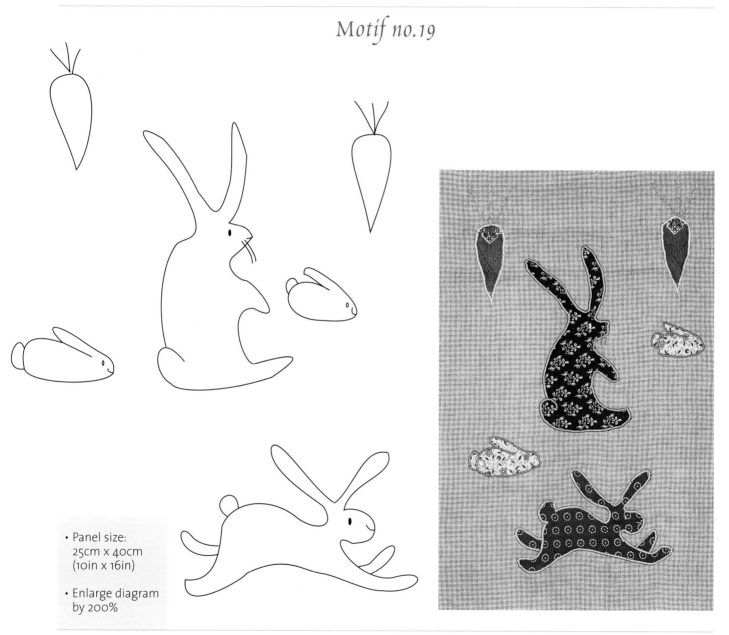

- Panel size:
  25cm x 40cm
  (10in x 16in)

- Enlarge diagram
  by 200%

RABBITS REVERSED

Motif no.20

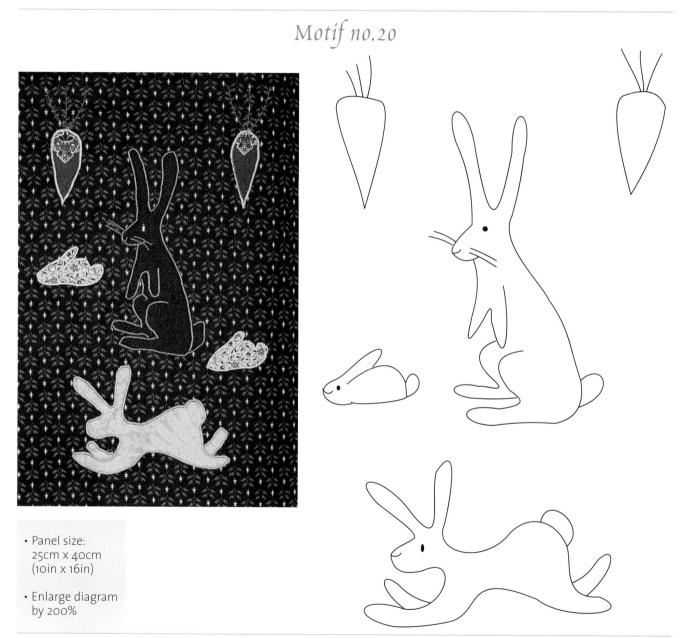

- Panel size:
  25cm x 40cm
  (10in x 16in)

- Enlarge diagram
  by 200%

PIGEONS

Motif no.21

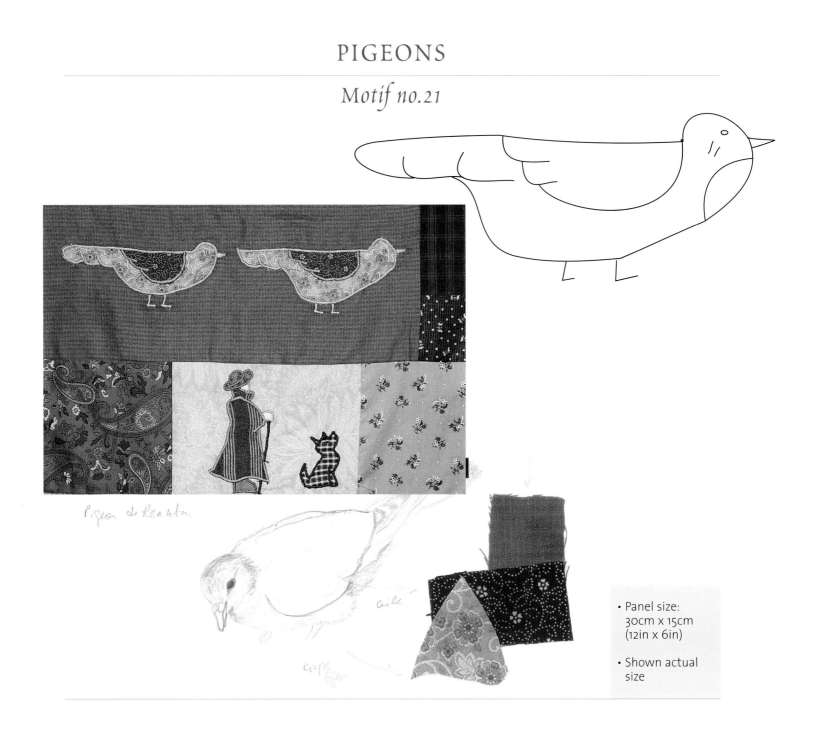

Pigeon & Renata

aile

corps pigeon

- Panel size:
  30cm x 15cm
  (12in x 6in)

- Shown actual
  size

MAN AND HIS DOG

Motif no.22

- Panel size:
  15cm x 10cm
  (6in x 4in)

- Shown actual size

DUCKS

Motif no.23

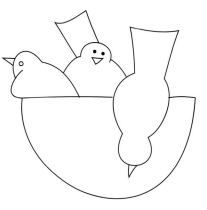

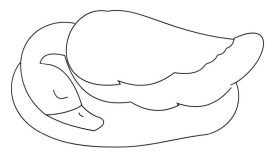

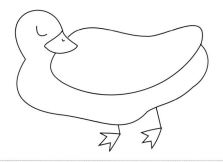

- Panel size:
  25cm x 40cm
  (10in x 16in)

- Enlarge diagram
  by 200%

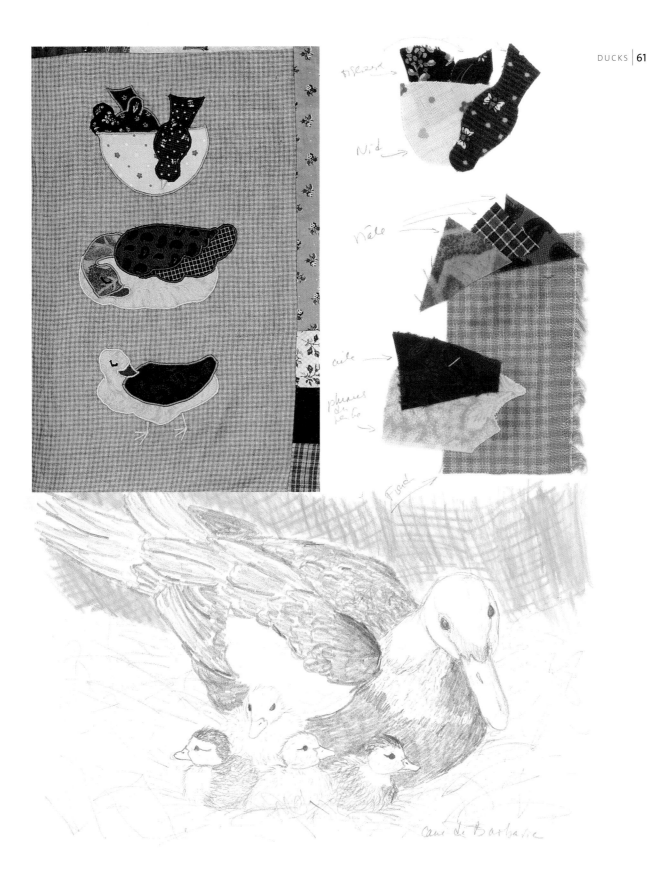

ROOSTER

Motif no.24

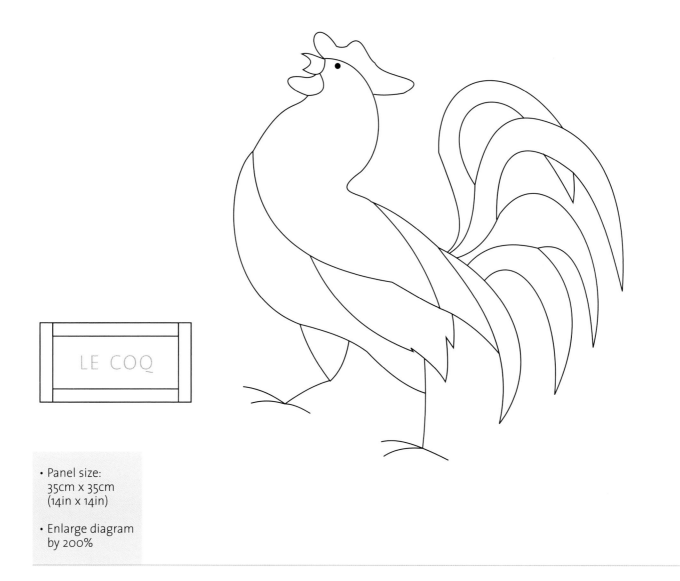

LE COQ

- Panel size:
35cm x 35cm
(14in x 14in)

- Enlarge diagram
by 200%

GEESE

Motif no.25

• Panel size:
 30cm x 30cm
 (12in x 12in)

• Enlarge diagram
 by 200%

GOATS

Motif no.26

- Panel size:
  30cm x 35cm
  (12in x 14in)

- Enlarge diagram
  by 200%

Poitrine

Bouc

chèvre

chevreau

Étiquette brodée

Bidon de lait

LES CHEVRES

LAIT LAIT LAIT

SOW AND HER YOUNG

Motif no.27

- Panel size:
  45cm x 30cm
  (18in x 12in)

- Enlarge diagram
  by 200%

Fond

Maman Cochon

petits Cochons

Large White

THREE HENS

Motif no.28

• Panel size:
35cm x 15cm
(14in x 6in)

• Shown actual
size

COWS

Motif no.29

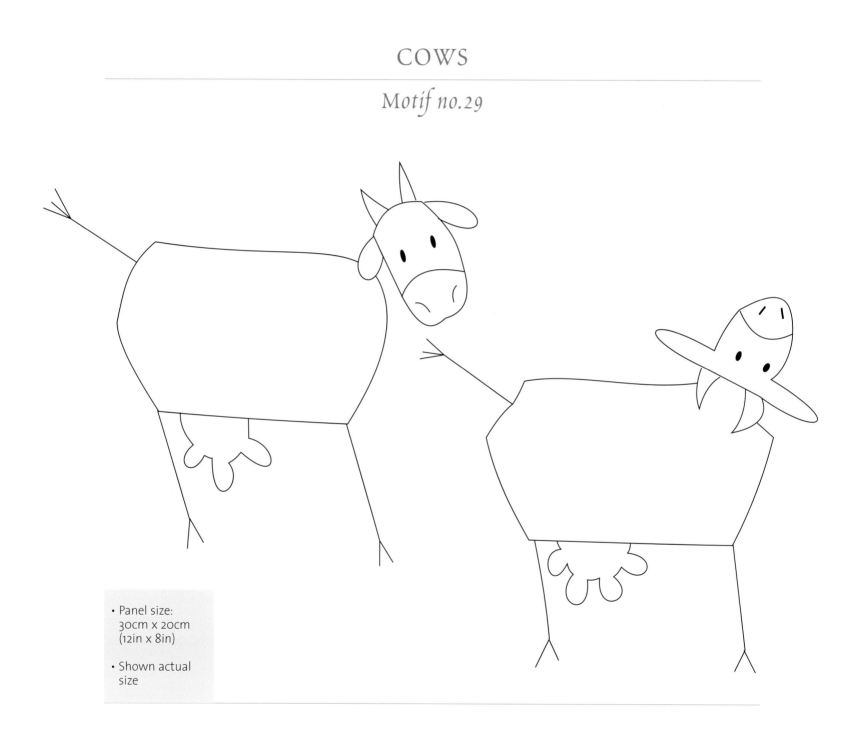

- Panel size:
  30cm x 20cm
  (12in x 8in)

- Shown actual
  size

THREE CATS

Motif no.30

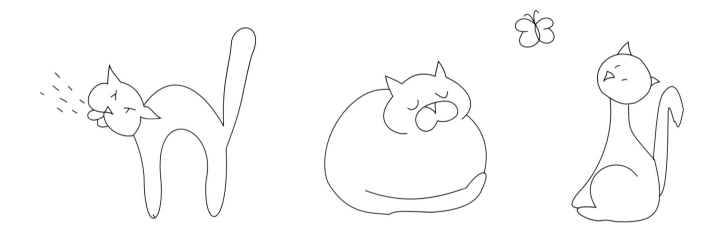

- Panel size:
  40cm x 15cm
  (16in x 6in)

- Enlarge diagram
  by 200%

MOTIFS FOR FILLER STRIPS

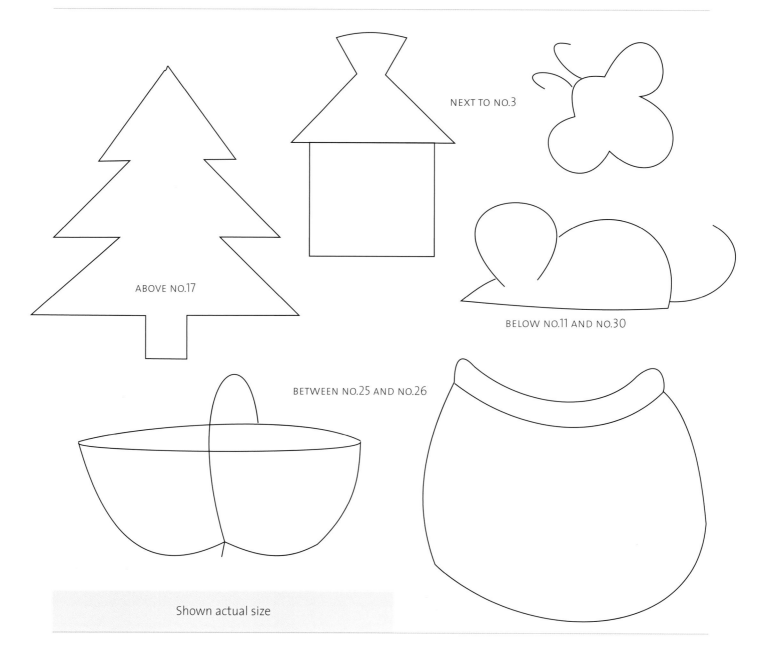

NEXT TO NO.3

ABOVE NO.17

BELOW NO.11 AND NO.30

BETWEEN NO.25 AND NO.26

Shown actual size

CORNER SQUARES

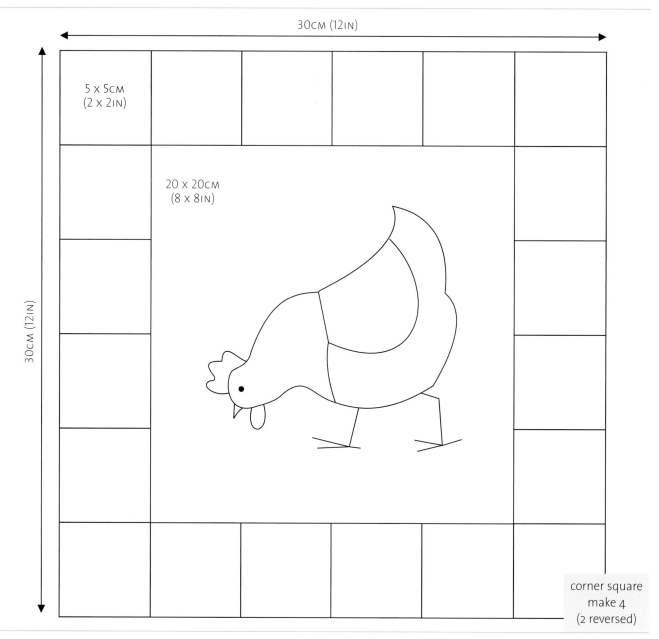

30cm (12in)

30cm (12in)

5 x 5cm
(2 x 2in)

20 x 20cm
(8 x 8in)

corner square
make 4
(2 reversed)

FOUR CORNER HENS

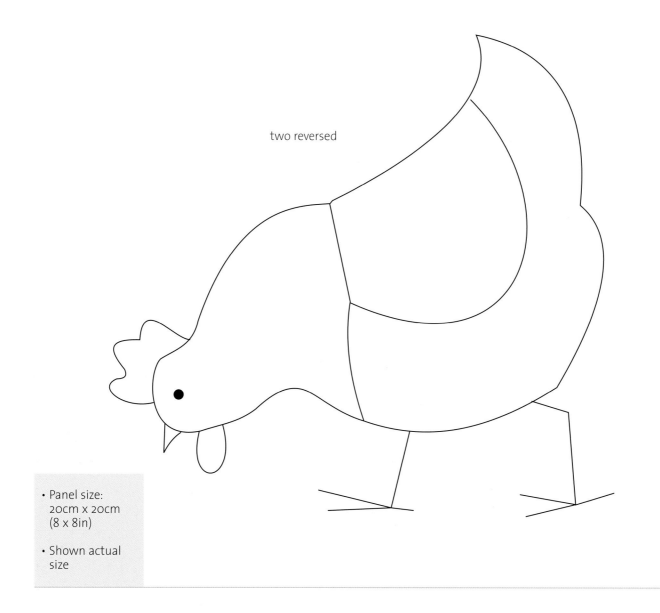

two reversed

- Panel size:
  20cm x 20cm
  (8 x 8in)

- Shown actual
  size

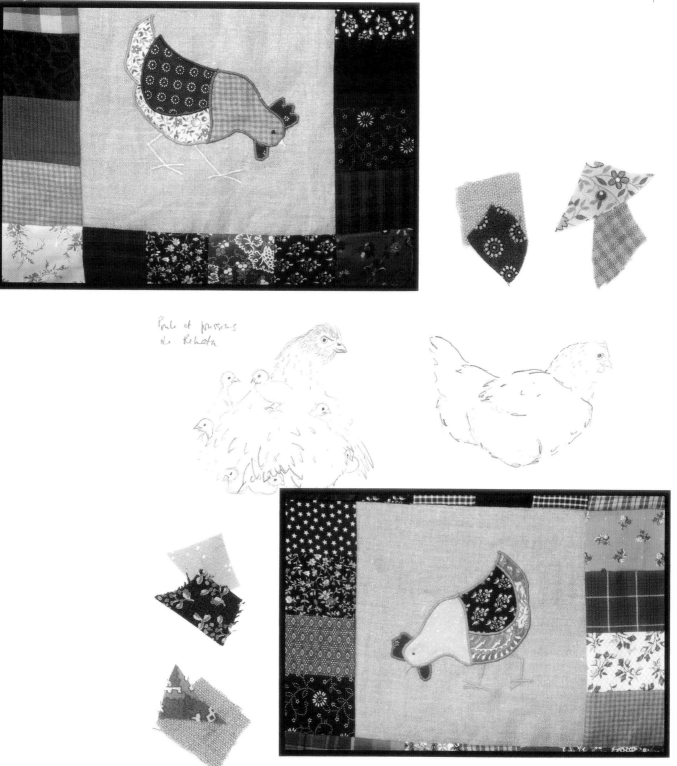

Poule et poussins
de Renata

MAKING UP THE
CENTRE PATCHWORK PANEL

MATERIALS, CUTTING OUT AND STITCHING INSTRUCTIONS

FINISHED QUILT DIMENSIONS: 2.5M X 2.5M (8FT 4IN X 8FT 4IN)

Materials required

- A selection of check, plaid and floral mini-print cotton fabrics for patchwork squares (see below for amounts).
- Cotton fabrics in blues, browns and yellows and so on for backing panels (see opposite for amounts).
- Cotton offcuts for the appliqué motifs.
- Unbleached linen for edge panels A, B, C and D and corner squares (see opposite for amount).
- Blue cotton for the quilt backing and border edgings E, F, G and H (see opposite for amount).
- Embroidery threads.
- 2.45m x 2.45m (8ft x 8ft) wadding.

Cutting out the fabric

(These measurements are given without seam allowances.)

Edge panels and border edgings

- 4 linen edge panels A, B, C and D: 30cm x 180cm (12in x 72in)
- 2 border edgings F and H: 5cm x 250cm (2in x 100in)
- 2 border edgings E and G: 5cm x 240cm (2in x 96in)

Patchwork squares

- 49 squares 10cm x 10cm (4in x 4in) – 2 with a bee motif
- 162 squares 5cm x 5cm (2in x 2in)
- 2 rectangles 5cm x 10cm (2in x 4in) – 1 with a hive motif
- 1 rectangle 5cm x 15cm (2in x 6in) – with a bee motif
- 2 rectangles 20cm x 5cm (8in x 2in)
- 2 rectangles 25cm x 5cm (10in x 2in)
- 1 rectangle 5cm x 30cm (2in x 12in)
- 1 rectangle 5cm x 30cm (2in x 12in)
- 3 rectangles 40cm x 5cm (16in x 2in) – 2 with four mice
- 1 rectangle 20cm x 10cm (8in x 4in) – with two fir trees

Instructions

➤ Start by working on the panels appliquéd with animal motifs. Trace or photocopy the designs, making sure that they are the correct size – several of the motifs need enlarging by 200%. Create templates and cut them out in the fabrics of your choice.

➤ Lay the pieces on to the appropriate size backing fabric panel and appliqué them using machine satin stitch or slipstitch by hand. Lastly, hand- or machine-embroider the details on the panel.

➤ Refer to the diagrams on page 89 for the order of stitching the patchwork squares and rectangles into strips before stitching them to the appliquéd panels.

➤ Make up the appliquéd panels and squares into larger panels in three steps as shown on page 87.

➤ Assemble these three panels to make up the square central section of your quilt.

➤ Make four corner squares (see page 78).

➤ Embroider and appliqué edge panels A, B, C and D following the instructions given on pages 96–120. Make up the corner panels (see step 4, page 121).

➤ Using the diagram as an aid, assemble the various completed sections (see step 5, page 121).

1.4m (55in) wide fabric amounts for edge panels, corner squares, border edgings and quilt backing

1.1m (44in) wide fabric amounts for backing panels

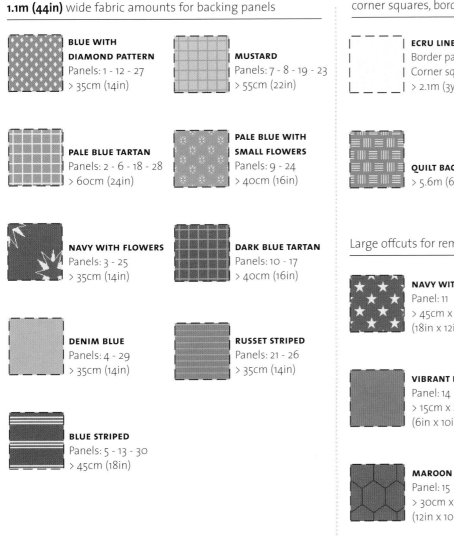

BLUE WITH DIAMOND PATTERN
Panels: 1 - 12 - 27
> 35cm (14in)

MUSTARD
Panels: 7 - 8 - 19 - 23
> 55cm (22in)

PALE BLUE TARTAN
Panels: 2 - 6 - 18 - 28
> 60cm (24in)

PALE BLUE WITH SMALL FLOWERS
Panels: 9 - 24
> 40cm (16in)

NAVY WITH FLOWERS
Panels: 3 - 25
> 35cm (14in)

DARK BLUE TARTAN
Panels: 10 - 17
> 40cm (16in)

DENIM BLUE
Panels: 4 - 29
> 35cm (14in)

RUSSET STRIPED
Panels: 21 - 26
> 35cm (14in)

BLUE STRIPED
Panels: 5 - 13 - 30
> 45cm (18in)

ECRU LINEN
Border panels
Corner squares
> 2.1m (3yd)

QUILT BACKING
> 5.6m (6yd 6in)

Large offcuts for remaining backing panels

NAVY WITH STARS
Panel: 11
> 45cm x 30cm
(18in x 12in)

NAVY WITH FLOWERS
Panel: 16
> 25cm x 25cm
(10in x 10in)

VIBRANT BLUE
Panel: 14
> 15cm x 25cm
(6in x 10in)

DARK GREEN
Panel: 20
> 30cm x 45cm
(12in x 18in)

MAROON
Panel: 15
> 30cm x 25cm
(12in x 10in)

STRAW YELLOW
Panel: 22
> 20cm x 15cm
(8in x 6in)

Use mainly cotton fabrics for your appliqué pieces; wool and synthetics can be used with care for special effects.

Diagram for assembling the central panel

Note: All measurements given in centimetres. Refer to motif templates (pages 18–81) for Imperial measurements.

Step 1: **A**

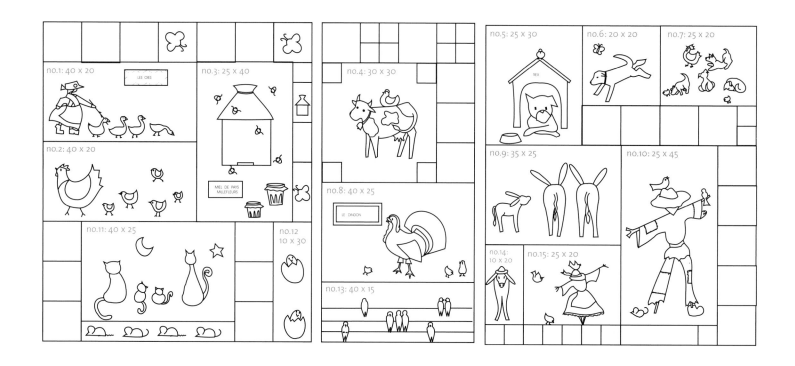

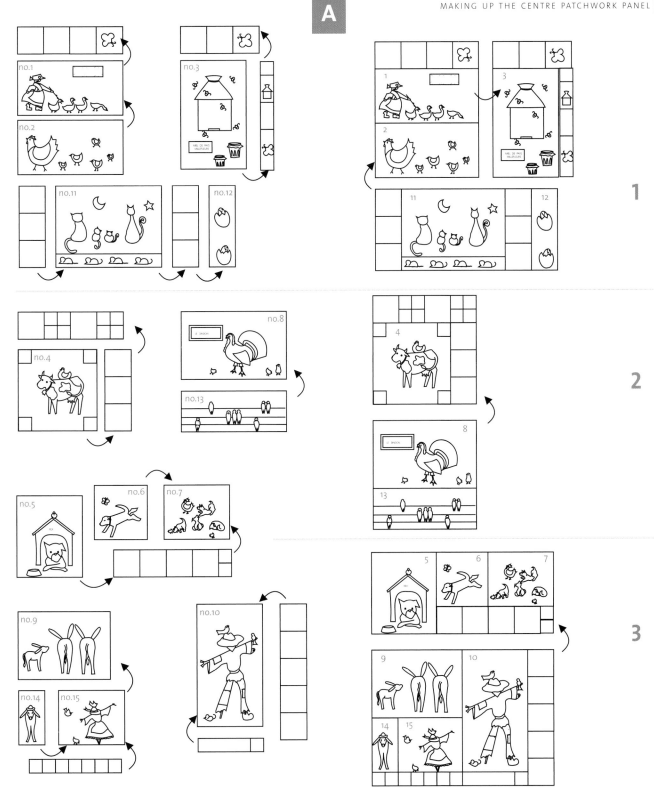

Step 2: **B**

B

1

2

3

4

Step 3: **C**

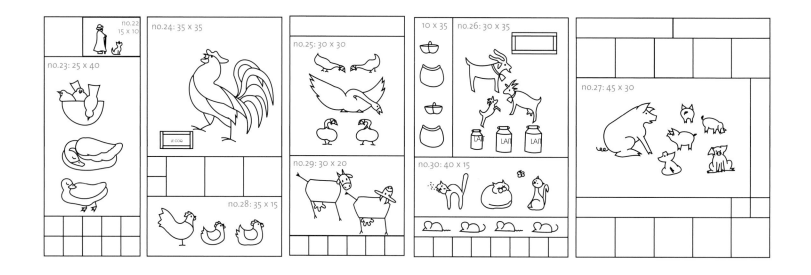

C

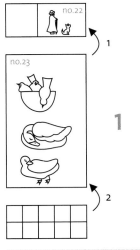

1

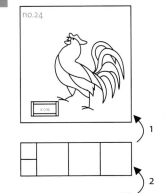

2

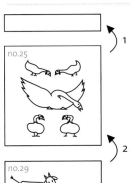

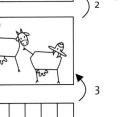

3

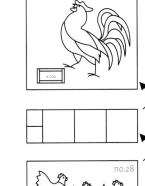

4

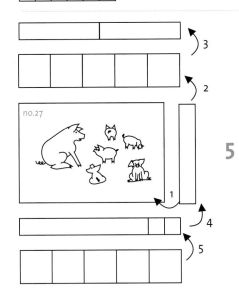

5

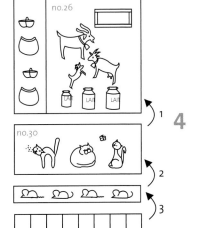

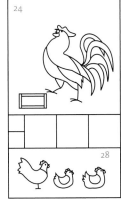

MAKING UP
THE BORDER PANELS

Border **A**

Border **A**

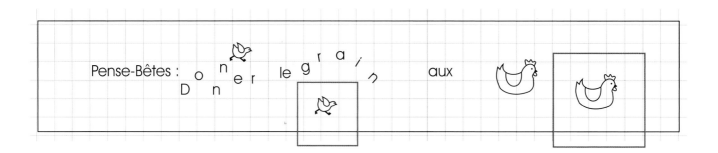

Pense-Bêtes : Donner le grain aux

scale:
1 square =
5cm (2in)

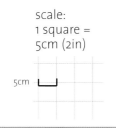

5cm

Embroider using a satin zigzag stitch

· Shown actual size

X 2

X 2

Border **B**

Border **B**

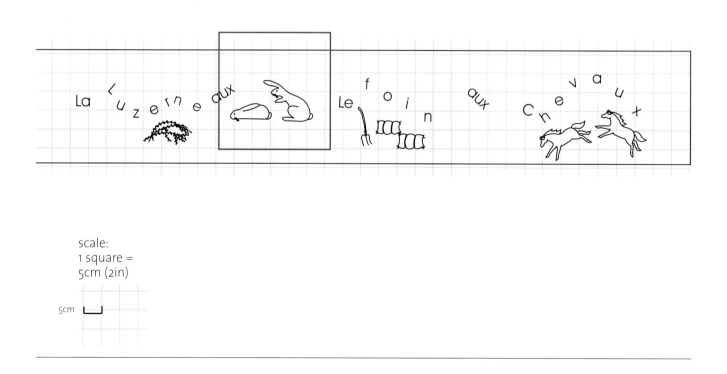

scale:
1 square =
5cm (2in)

5cm

Border **B**

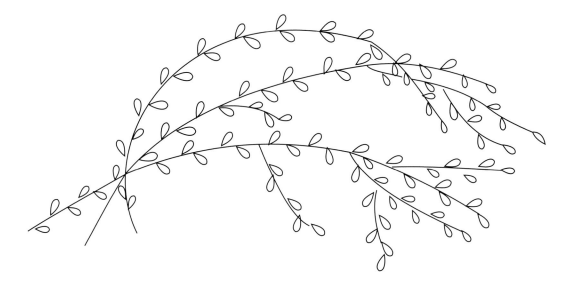

Embroider by
hand or using
a machine

• Shown actual
  size

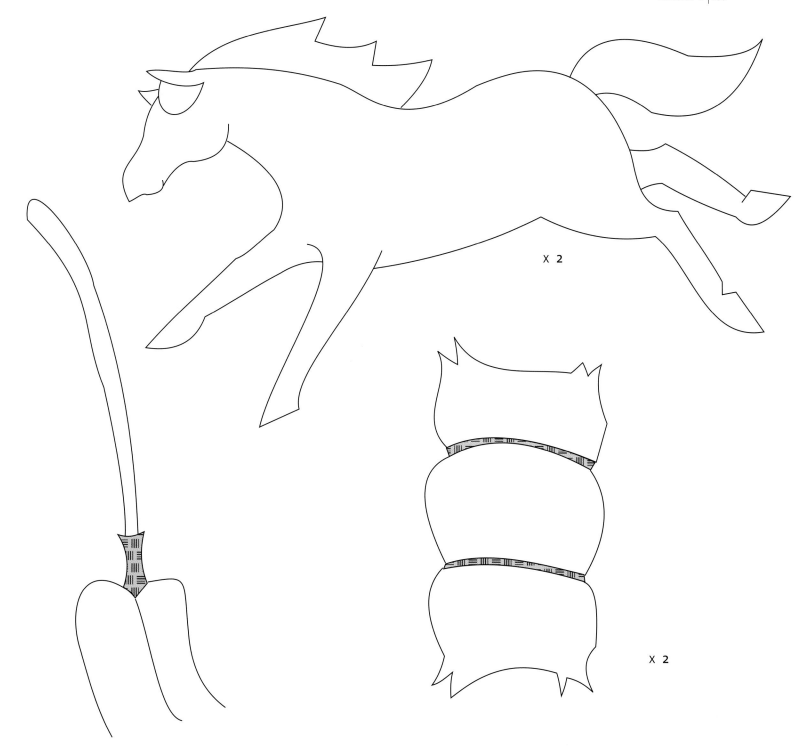

X 2

X 2

Border **C**

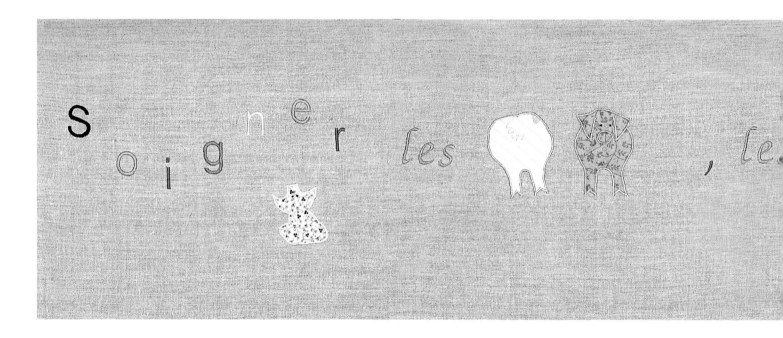

Border **C**

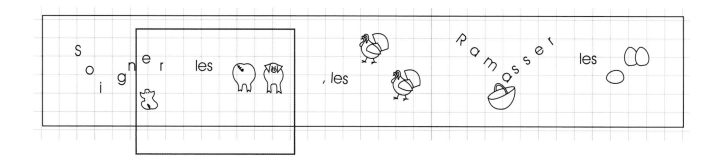

scale:
1 square =
5cm (2in)

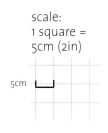

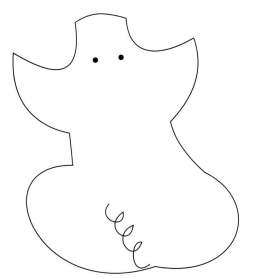

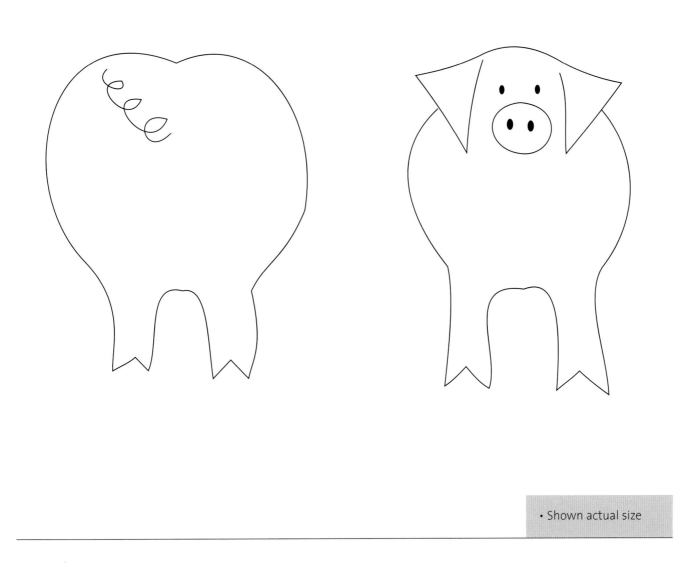

• Shown actual size

Border **C**

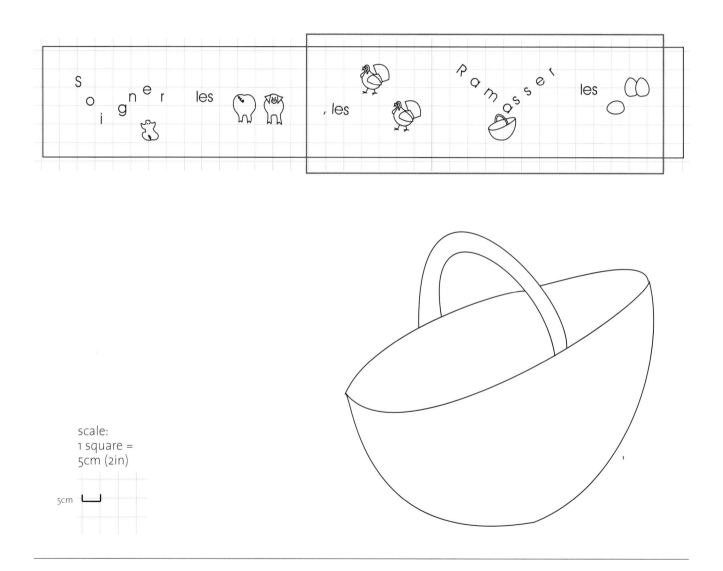

scale:
1 square =
5cm (2in)

5cm

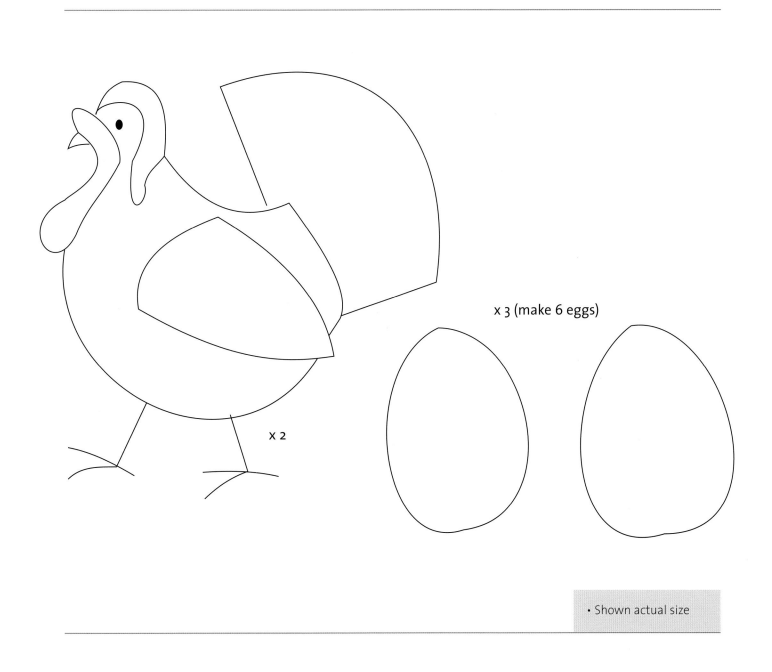

x 3 (make 6 eggs)

x 2

• Shown actual size

Border **D**

Border **D**

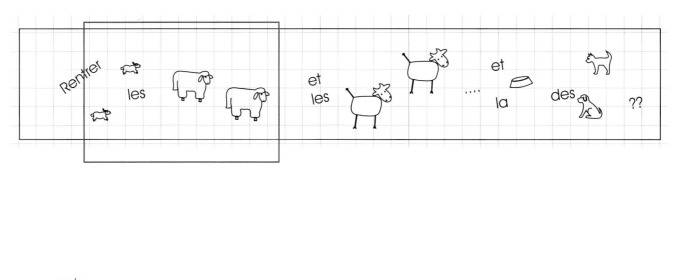

scale:
1 square =
5cm (2in)

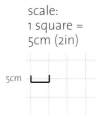

5cm

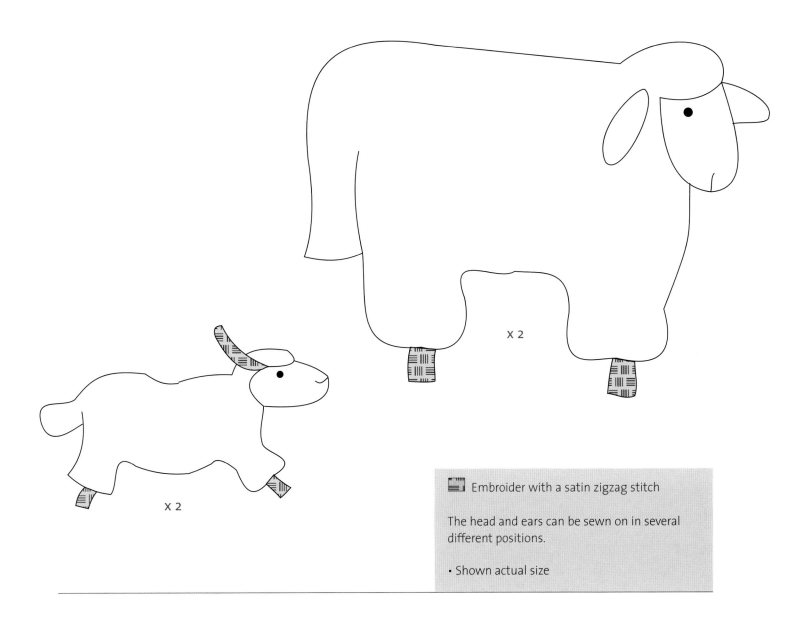

Embroider with a satin zigzag stitch

The head and ears can be sewn on in several different positions.

• Shown actual size

X 2

X 2

Border **D**

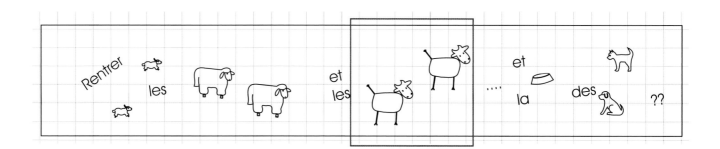

scale:
1 square =
5cm (2in)

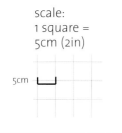

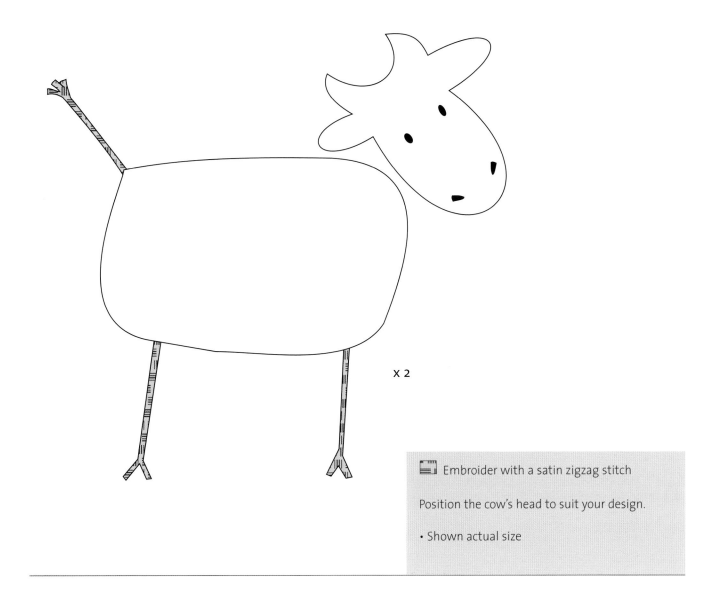

X 2

Embroider with a satin zigzag stitch

Position the cow's head to suit your design.

• Shown actual size

Border **D**

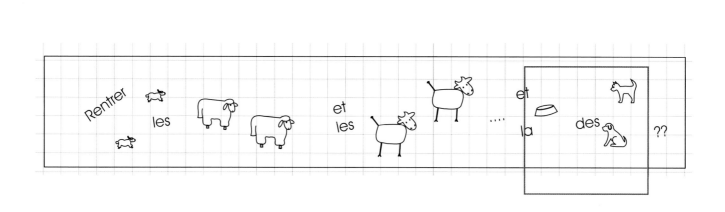

scale:
1 square =
5cm (2in)

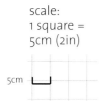

5cm

🖼 Embroider with a satin
zigzag stitch

• Shown actual size

Assembling the borders

Follow steps 4 and 5 opposite to assemble the border panels. The numbered arrows give the order in which the pieces should be sewn together.

ALTERNATIVE METHODS FOR WORKING THE FOUR LINEN BORDERS

Embroidered letters
The words are machine-embroidered but if you do not have access to a machine, or if you find it easier, you can use stem stitch or satin stitch to embroider them by hand. Alternatively, why not cut the letters out from offcuts of fabric and appliqué them on to the borders?

Appliqué motifs
If you have difficulty pivoting the fabric as you appliqué the motifs because of the length of the panels why not appliqué your animals on to shorter lengths of backing material and then stitch them together? You will need to add seam allowances to the original measurements.

Lining your quilt

Lay out the backing fabric, wrong side up, cover with the wadding and then put the quilt, right side up, on top. Pin the three layers together, starting from the centre and working out to the centre of each edge. Then pin round the edge, setting the pins at right angles to the edge and about 15cm (6in) apart. Fold the edges to the back of the quilt, pin, tack and then sew a neat hem. To keep the three layers together you can stitch along the lines of the panels.

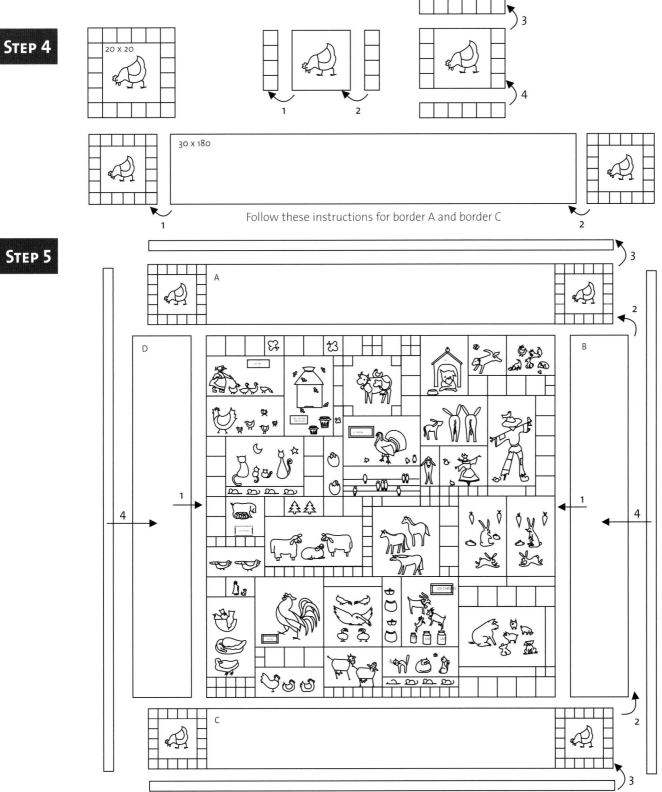

STEP 4

20 X 20

1   2

3

4

30 x 180

Follow these instructions for border A and border C

1   2

STEP 5

3

A

2

D   B

1   1

4   4

2

C

2

3

CHAPTER V
OTHER PROJECTS

OTHER WAYS TO USE THE MOTIFS

Listed here are suggestions for projects that allow you to make use of the motifs and designs in this book without having to make a large quilt.

1. Cushions

These cushions provide the perfect finishing touch to a country-style interior and would complement your bedspread.

Motif worked on 20cm x 20cm (8in x 8in) background panel with 5cm (2in) patchwork squares

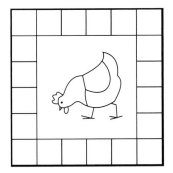

The corner hens (see page 78–80) make fun cushions. Make a pair, reversing one motif.

Linen would work well as a background fabric: you could choose the other colours to match your interior décor.

Why not make up a series of cushions featuring other animals? You could adapt the size of the motifs to fit the size of the background panel, or add other animals.

Motif worked on 35cm x 35cm (14in x 14in) background panel with 5cm (2in) patchwork squares

For the larger cushion use the cow (motif no.4), turkey (motif no.8), horses (motif no.18), or rooster (motif no.24) .

2. Bedside rug

Motifs worked on 60cm x 50cm (24in x 20in) background panel with 10cm (4in) wide borders

Suggestions for colours:

- Background panel in unbleached linen
- Cats in a blue print (motif no.11)
- Russet mice (filler motifs page 76)
- Border in blue and brown plaid or checks

Many of the quilt motifs can be used in this kind of composition. Why not have as your theme hens bordered by chicks, cows or goats with milk churns, pigs and piglets, rabbits dreaming about carrots or a pair of turkeys with a border of Christmas trees?

3. Rex the dog bedside rug

Motif worked on a 25cm x 30cm (10in x 12in) panel with patchwork borders 105cm x 90cm (40in x 36in)

This small quilt has a single central motif which can be adapted to fit the size of the background panel. You can increase the size of this panel as indicated by the red lines, allowing you to be creative and use other designs. The patchwork squares and borders are 5cm or 10cm (2in or 4in) wide with the corner paw prints set in 15cm (6in) squares.

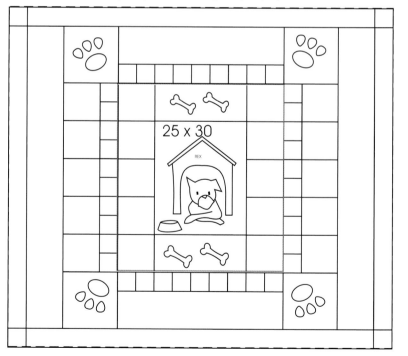

Two further suggestions for the central panel

Plan a small quilt round your chosen central panel using graph paper and keeping the patchwork squares and borders to multiples of 5cm or 10cm (2in or 4in).

Suggestion 1:
Adapt the dog rug using the rooster in the central panel and sew hens into the corners instead of paw prints.

Suggestion 2:
Place the scarecrow in the centre and sew birds down the side panels or place them in corner squares.

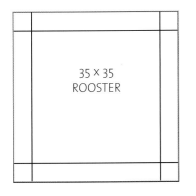

4. Small themed quilt

Finished quilt measures 1.3m (52in) square with borders and patchwork squares of 5cm or 10cm (2in or 4in) wide

FEATHERED FRIENDS!

This quilt uses some of the bird motifs and backgrounds from the large quilt. You could also make a farmyard animals quilt.

Plan your design on a sheet of 5mm (¹/₄in) squared paper where each square represents 5cm (2in).

Draw an outline measuring 26 x 26 squares and an inner square measuring 24 x 24 squares which will leave a 5cm border. Position the panel backgrounds and their motifs inside the border. Link everything together using 5cm or 10cm (2in or 4in) squares.

You can create a smaller or larger quilt in the same way.

If this seems too complicated, why not have a go at the next project, the easy-to-make quilt?

5. Easy-to-make quilt

Finished quilt measures 1.4m x 1.75m (56in x 70in) with motifs worked on 30cm (12in) square background panels with 5cm or 10cm (2in or 4in) wide borders

For this quilt the motifs are appliquéd on to backgrounds of the same size. You could make each panel a different colour – the choice is yours!

Suggestions for motifs:

- Use a selection of the motifs given for the large quilt.
- Select one or two motifs and repeat them in different colours (scarecrows, sheep, cats and so on).
- Use the motifs and lettering from the border panels of the large quilt.
- Limit yourself to a theme: birds, farm animals, cats and dogs and so on.

Suggestions for sizes:

- Make a quilt of only 4, 6 or 8 panels.
- Make a quilt with smaller panels, 25cm or 20cm (10in or 8in) square.

Always draw your design out on squared paper before starting work.

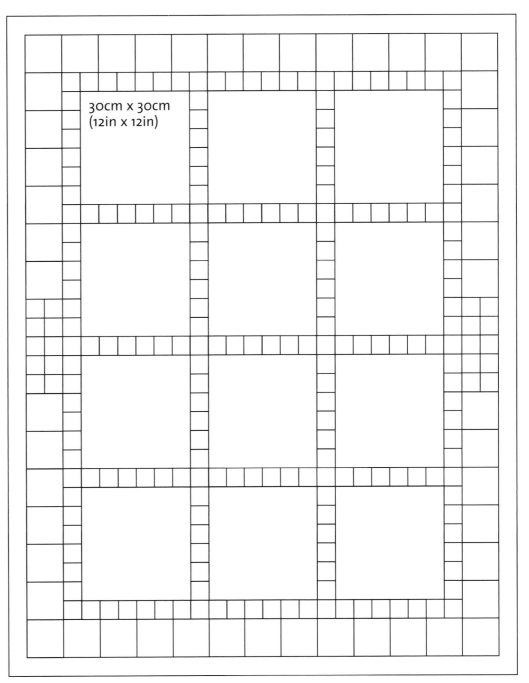

30cm x 30cm
(12in x 12in)

Notes